W9-BMZ-836

Festivals of the World

MADAGASCAR

Gareth Stevens Publishing
MILWAUKEE

Written by
ROYSTON ELLIS AND JOHN R. JONES

Edited by
AUDREY LIM

Designed by
LYNN CHIN

Picture research by
SUSAN JANE MANUEL

First published in North America in 1999 by
Gareth Stevens Publishing
1555 North RiverCenter Drive, Suite 201
Milwaukee, Wisconsin 53212 USA

For a free color catalog describing Gareth Stevens'
list of high-quality books and multimedia
programs, call
1-800-542-2595 (USA)
or 1-800-461-9120 (Canada).
Gareth Stevens Publishing's Fax: (414) 225-0377.
See our catalog, too, on the World Wide Web:
http://gsinc.com

© TIMES EDITIONS PTE LTD 1999
Originated and designed by
Times Books International
an imprint of Times Editions Pte Ltd
Times Centre, 1 New Industrial Road
Singapore 536196
Printed in Singapore

Library of Congress Cataloging-in-Publication Data:
Ellis, Royston.
Madagascar / by Royston Ellis and John R. Jones.
p. cm.—(Festivals of the world)
Includes bibliographical references and index.
Summary: Describes how the culture of Madagascar
is reflected in its many festivals, including
Gasytsara, Alahamady Be, and Hira Gasy.
ISBN 0-8368-2023-1 (1ib. bdg.)
1. Festivals—Madagascar—Juvenile literature.
2. Madagascar—Social life and customs—Juvenile
literature. [1. Festivals—Madagascar. 2. Holidays—
Madagascar. 3. Madagascar—Social life and
customs.] I. Jones, John R. II. Title. III. Series.
GT4889.M4E44   1999
394.269691—dc21   98-41783

1 2 3 4 5 6 7 8 9 03 02 01 00 99

CONTENTS

It's Festival Time . . .

Come see Madagascar's exciting festivals. On Fridays, the *Zoma* [zo-MA] take place. It is the second biggest open-air market festival in the world. On Sundays, the *Hira Gasy* [EE-ra GA-ssy] festival of storytelling, music, and dancing is **spellbinding**. The most unusual festival of all is *Famadihana* [fa-ma-DEE-an] where people dance with their dead relatives' bones. It's festival time in Madagascar . . .

WHERE'S MADAGASCAR?

Madagascar is the fourth largest island in the world. Its nearest neighbors are the islands of Réunion and Mauritius to the east and the Comoro Islands and the African country of Mozambique to the west. More distant

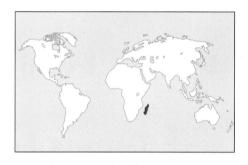

neighbors are the Seychelles, a group of islands to the northeast, and Antarctica to the south. Madagascar's capital is Antananarivo, meaning "Town of a thousand warriors."

Who are the Malagasy?

Madagascar's original inhabitants were from Indonesia and Malaysia. Africans arrived later and settled on the lowlands. In the ninth century, Arab colonists arrived. They were followed by the Portuguese in 1528 and British merchants in 1600. In 1896, Madagascar became a French colony but became independent in 1960. Today, there are 18 different cultural groups in Madagascar, the largest being the Merina, followed by the Betsimisaraka.

Madagascar's economy is mostly agricultural. The Malagasy are cheerful and industrious.

4

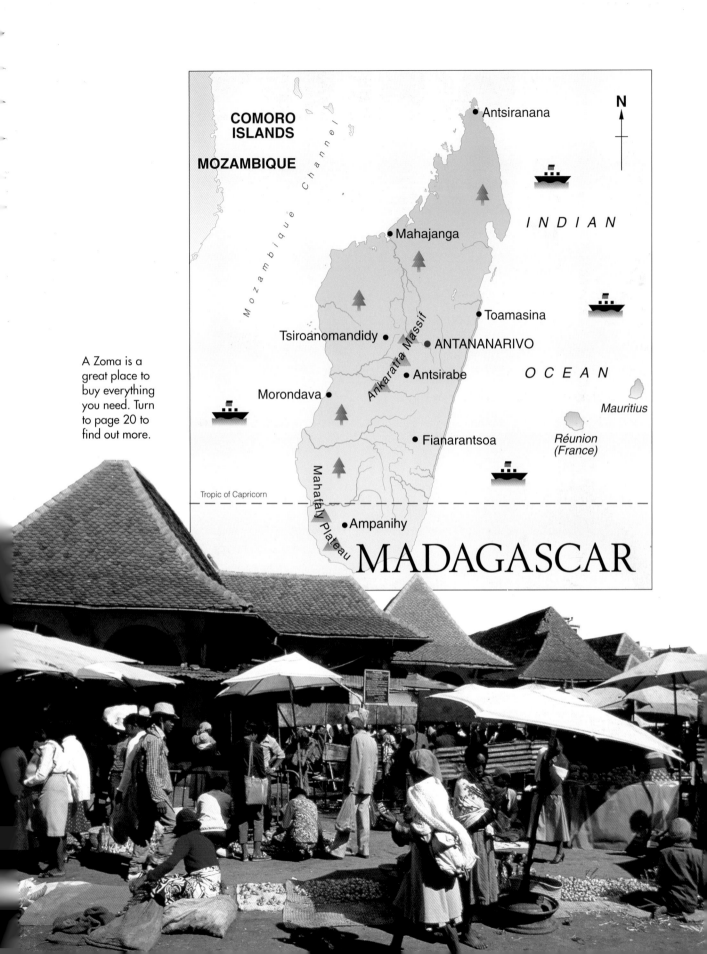

COMORO
ISLANDS

MOZAMBIQUE

N

● Antsiranana

Mozambique Channel

INDIAN

● Mahajanga

● Toamasina

Tsiroanomandidy ●

Ankaratra Massif

● ANTANANARIVO

OCEAN

● Antsirabe

Morondava ●

Mauritius

● Fianarantsoa

*Réunion
(France)*

Tropic of Capricorn

Mahafaly Plateau

● Ampanihy

MADAGASCAR

A Zoma is a
great place to
buy everything
you need. Turn
to page 20 to
find out more.

WHEN'S THE PARTY?

SPRING

- ✪ **ALL SAINTS' DAY**
- ✪ **GASYTSARA**—A contemporary music and dance festival that usually occurs in late spring. Tribes play traditional dance rhythms using stringed instruments, whistles, guitars, and flutes. The music is often accompanied by hand-clapping.

Want to read more about Sambatra? Turn to page 10 for more information.

SUMMER

- ✪ **CHRISTMAS**—Christ's birth is celebrated on December 25th.
- ✪ **REPUBLIC DAY**—Parades are held in the capital city of Antananarivo and other large towns. A big reception is held at Antananarivo for important political dignitaries.
- ✪ **NEW YEAR'S DAY**

AUTUMN

- **ALAHAMADY BE**—In March, families enjoy special festive food and drinks to mark the beginning of the Malagasy New Year.
- **SANTABARY**—Celebrates the first rice harvest in April.
- **HOLY WEEK**—Catholics hold processions and church services in the week leading up to Easter Sunday.
- **EASTER MONDAY**
- **LABOR DAY**—A holiday honoring workers. Politicians and workers' leaders make speeches.
- **ASCENSION DAY**

WINTER

- **ZOMA**
- **FAMADIHANA**
- **SAMBATRA**
- **HIRA GASY**
- **BETROTHAL FESTIVALS**

Malagasy food is great! Turn to pages 30 and 31 and learn how to make a refreshing fruit drink.

FAMILY FESTIVALS

Family bonds are important to the Malagasy, and they have two festivals, in particular, that families celebrate together: *Alahamady Be* [a-lah-ha-MAAD BAY], or the New Year, and *Sambatra* [sahm BAT]. Read on to find out more!

Off to a good start

Alahamady Be is a day when family members and friends get together to celebrate the beginning of another year. People feast, exchange gifts, and sing hymns.

Alahamady Be is celebrated when the first new moon in the first month of the year appears in March. People in Antananarivo enjoy this two-day festival tremendously. They put on their best clothes, which are usually brightly colored.

On New Year's Eve, families make their way to the sacred royal hill of Ambohimanga, reveling in loud, boisterous music. When they reach the hill, the families gather around what was previously the Queen's Palace and pray to their ancestors.

These Malagasy are ready to celebrate the New Year. Notice their bright, beautiful clothes!

Feasts and hymns

After prayers are over, families enjoy many special festive foods. One such food is *romazava* [ROO-ma-ZAAV], Madagascar's national meat dish. It is flavored with herbs and leaves and served with rice, known as *vary* [VAR]. People also eat their fill of smoked sausages, vegetables, and **zebu** meat. Adults enjoy wine made from cane sugar and rice. Throughout the feasting, families take the opportunity to find out how their friends and extended family are doing.

On New Year's Day, people greet the morning with a Christian hymn. It is common for the Malagasy to combine Christian beliefs with traditional customs and practices.

Above: People make their way up the sacred hill of Ambohimanga.

Below: Everyone wants to be part of the celebrations.

Left: Will there be space for everyone?

Sambatra

The **circumcision** festival, Sambatra, is celebrated with gaiety and festivities. The Malagasy consider children treasured gifts from God, and families commonly have as many as 10 children.

In Madagascar, boys are circumcised at about five years of age. There are taboos, or *fady* [FAH-di], about not being circumcised. For example, uncircumcised males cannot be buried in the family tomb. Also, uncircumcised males are not considered "men" and are not allowed to marry.

Below: Having many children stems from the belief that the more children a person has, the more that person is blessed.

The actual event

The circumcision ceremony is an exciting event for both the young boy and his family. Many relatives accompany the boy to the hospital, all piling into cars or *taxi-brousses* [TAK-si-BROOSSES], which are small pick-up trucks. After the circumcision procedure, the young boy returns home and rests in bed for a few days while his family celebrates.

The day of circumcision is the day young boys become men. It has great significance and is an occasion for much rejoicing. All the boy's relatives attend this celebration, bringing with them an envelope containing money that will help the boy in his adult life. The family enjoys a great feast, and there is often music and dancing that continue throughout the day.

An enthusiastic group of party-goers celebrates a relative's circumcision

Think about this

Many cultures practice circumcision, but the age of circumcision varies. In Kenya, the Maasai tribe circumcises boys when they are around 15 years old. Ethiopians circumcise male offspring either shortly after birth or within a few years of birth. The ancient Egyptians circumcised boys between six and twelve years of age.

REMEMBERING ANCESTORS

The Malagasy believe that a relative who passes away assumes the status of an ancestor. Ancestors are very important to the Malagasy because they believe ancestors have the authority to affect disasters and bring good fortune. So, ancestors are highly respected and even worshiped. To worship their ancestors, the Malagasy often have joyous celebrations, sometimes throwing a party at the relative's funeral or having an **exhumation** festival. Does this sound intriguing? Read more about it on the following pages!

Women on their way to a celebration. Look at their amazing sense of balance!

The farewell party

Above: Music is an essential part of Malagasy celebrations.

A send-off party is very much a family affair. A few days before the funeral, relatives arrive bringing food and drink. Countless village members attend the celebration and listen to the village leader deliver a long, profound speech, called *kabary* [ka-BAHR]. If the deceased relative was a rich person, guests enjoy a tasty zebu feast. The deceased is wrapped in burial cloth, given a new name, and taken to a magnificent tomb. Merrymakers dance around the tomb and enjoy the party atmosphere. If you are wondering how funeral partying started, one old Malagasy legend says that, when King Tsiampody died, thousands of subjects came to give him a grand farewell party and even feasted on zebu meat. For another Malagasy legend explaining the funeral party, turn to page 27.

A Malagasy tomb is beautifully decorated. The Malagasy believe that a tomb is for eternity, but a house is just for a lifetime.

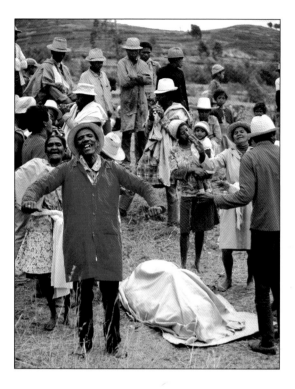

Famadihana

The Malagasy do not worship their ancestors only at funerals but also at Famadihana. This festival is celebrated by the Merina in the dry, cold winter months between June and September. It is a time of great exuberance and joy, when dead relatives are removed from their tombs to be the guests of honor at a celebration held especially for them. This traditional festival dates back many decades. Today, people are prepared to borrow money to ensure that the party is a memorable one. The Merina believe it is important to be on good terms with their relatives, even after those relatives have passed away.

Above and *below:* Famadihana is full of rejoicing and dancing.

Living it up

The night before Famadihana, many relatives visit the tomb of an ancestor. They walk around it in a zig-zag fashion, often sprinkling rum on it and shouting to the dead person inside that the next day will be a day to remember. Early the next day, a joyful procession winds its way to the tomb, headed by a master of ceremonies dressed in a red coat. Sprinkling rum or whiskey near the western entrance of the tomb, he gives orders for it to be opened. A group of men enter the vault and carry out the bones of the deceased that have been put in a bag. The bones are dusted and placed in a new blue burial cloth, called *lamba mena* [LAM-ba MEN].

The party's just begun

The relatives of the deceased take the bones to the ancestor's former home, where a great welcome awaits. No expense has been spared for a huge feast prepared in honor of the dead. Relatives can hardly contain their excitement as the bones are set down on a plaited mat. As they feast on zebu, turkey, ox, or chicken meat and drink fruity Malagasy wine, they tell the ancestor how happy they are to visit once more. Besides talking to the bones, relatives even hold them and dance with them. It is a wild and happy celebration.

Resting easy

As nightfall approaches, the deceased is taken back to the resting place, and the party comes to an end. The tomb's entrance is sealed again with mud, and the relatives are content and satisfied that they have looked after their ancestor well.

Think about this
The Malagasy also remember their dead with tomb decorations. These decorations are wooden slabs with delicately carved tops showing incidents in the life of the deceased. Many carvings are zebus, perhaps indicating the dead person was a zebu farmer. Often, drawings adorn the sides of the tomb, showing more examples of what the deceased's life was like.

HIRA GASY

Speech-making and music are regular parts of Malagasy life. Over the years, they have been formalized as a celebration known as Hira Gasy, which takes place every Sunday in Antananarivo and on special occasions.

Telling it like it is

Highly respected elders skilled in the art of **oratory** deliver expert speeches. Many Malagasy oratory experts come from Fianarantsoa. This form of storytelling is both entertaining and imaginative. The elder begins by giving advice and opinions, starting with modest words, building up with jokes and fables, then launching into encouragement on living a better life. The speech **extolls** the importance of the family, urging youngsters to respect their elders. It also emphasizes the importance of upholding Malagasy traditions. The speech becomes even more frenzied as the elder begins using proverbs to give advice. Many of these proverbs have simple themes and feature everyday life. The speech can go on for a long time, and the crowd responds enthusiastically.

A respected elder delivers a long speech on life and traditions.

A winning performance

Besides the elders giving impressive speeches, two colorfully dressed teams also compete against each other. Each team has 7 men and 18 women. The women wear long, bright pink nineteenth-century-style gowns and white **lambas** [LAM-bas]. A lamba is a type of shawl, or wrap worn by both men and women. The men are also smartly dressed, wearing red nineteenth-century-style French jackets, lamba wraps, and straw hats. The band leader has the privilege of wearing a distinctive blue jacket and usually plays a military-style drum. The celebrations are loud and raucous. They continue throughout the day, so many people in the audience bring along their own food and drink.

Above: Hira Gasy is a traditional celebration that features oratory and music.

The audience decides who the winners are.

Appreciating the music

The crowd judges the competition and expresses its appreciation with hand-clapping, shouting, and cheering. The women's leading singers burst into melodious, but sometimes slightly harsh, harmony, accompanied by a colorful band. Waving their hands about **frantically**, they attempt to win over the crowd by using very expressive gestures. The band's tempo increases as the crowd enthusiastically responds.

Above: Besides traditional instruments, the Malagasy also enjoy playing instruments from other cultures.

Banding together

All the while, band members try to impress the audience with their own distinctive and unique sense of rhythm. The traditional high-pitched Malagasy flute, or *sodina* [so-DEEN], can be heard despite loud drumming and percussion sounds. Other instruments include the trumpet, clarinet, and **valiha** [va-LEEB]. The valiha is a type of zither found in Indonesia and Malaysia. It has strings attached lengthwise around a hollow bamboo tube. The player plucks the strings like a harp.

A band member prepares for the competition.

Musical styles

Hira Gasy reflects the importance the Malagasy place on music. Malagasy men particularly enjoy singing folk songs and church hymns. A lot of traditional and contemporary music has its foundations in dance rhythms.

Music and singing are important in Malagasy culture.

Popular instruments

The Malagasy enjoy singing with musical accompaniment. Interestingly, however, many of their traditional instruments have only one note. The *kiloloka* [KEE-lo-LOOK], for example, produces a shrill whistle, and the sodina is loud and high-pitched. When each musician plays his or her single note together with a group, the result is a harmonious blend. Besides their traditional instruments, the Malagasy also favor drums, rattles, guitars, fiddles, and accordions.

Think about this
What do the Hira Gasy speech competitions remind you of? Have you ever been in a competition where you had to present your viewpoint and defend it when someone disagreed with you? These competitions are called debates.

19

ZOMA

Every Friday throughout the year, Antananarivo hosts one of the largest outdoor market **spectacles** in the world. This market festival is a celebration of everything Malagasy. On Zoma day, the entire length of Avenue de l'Independence and other hillside streets become a sea of **glistening** white umbrellas.

A stall holder displaying her goods at the Zoma.

An early start

The Malagasy prepare for this lively, colorful event the day before. Overloaded taxi-brousses, trucks, and handcarts **converge** on Antananarivo from all over Madagsacar. Well before sunrise, Merina traders have occupied every available inch (centimeter) of pavement. To ensure they have enough space to display their goods, these traders might even spend the night sleeping on the hard ground!

We're off to the Zoma! Come along and see all the things you can buy!

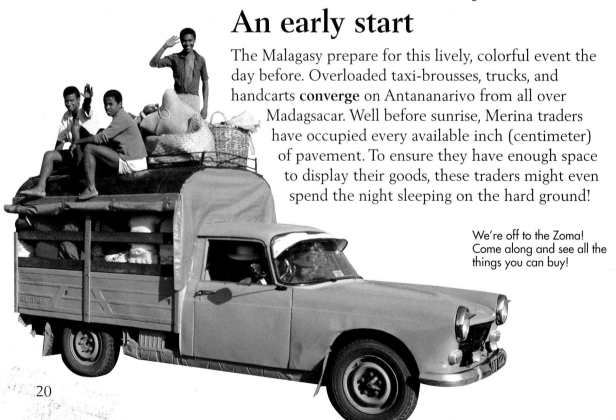

20

Anything and everything

For Zoma spectators, this colorful event is a chance to meet their friends, catch up on local gossip, and, for those who can afford it, buy something special. Along the crowded streets, people enjoy listening to Malagasy rock music as they take their time browsing through the wares each stall offers. Interesting smells invade the nostrils, and a rainbow of colors dazzles the eyes. Stalls sell grapes, strawberries, peaches, cherries, pears, apples, and even wild raspberries when they are in season. Women wearing lambas over their shoulders boil rice and brew coffee on tiny charcoal stoves. Some try to tempt onlookers with fresh French bread laced with honey. In the distance, you can hear an herbal tonic drink seller cry out, "Bitter, bitter," in Malagasy as he swings his long aluminium teapot and tiny mugs.

The Zoma is an exciting time for buyers and sellers alike and an opportunity to get a real bargain!

Magical cures

Western medicines are very expensive in Madagascar, so people usually choose herbal remedies instead. Zoma traders sell cures for anything, from babies' pimples to dogs' warts. Ground sage with water is a popular drink because the Malagasy believe it blesses the drinker with good luck. Basil is useful to keep away mosquitoes, which carry malaria, and the Malagasy believe it also can be taken orally to prevent bubonic plague. The Malagasy also believe that a silkworm cocoon with a live grub inside is an excellent remedy for stomach complaints, and they sell certain plant roots shaped like snakes as **tranquilizers**. The Zoma is, indeed, a place to find both the common and the exotic!

Right: A colorful display of food for sale.

Hunting for souvenirs

A festive welcome awaits tourist souvenir hunters. They are often offered a glass of sweet, fruity Malagasy wine while shopkeepers show them decorative tablecloths dotted with scenes of the Madagascar countryside. Few parents can resist buying their children flutes or whistles made of bamboo. Wood carvers selling unique zebu-drawn carts compete for business with hat sellers, leather workers, embroiderers, and mineral traders offering low-priced rock crystals, opals, and topaz. From locals to foreigners, everybody has a fantastic time at the Zoma.

Come to the Zoma and you'll be amazed by the sights, sounds, and smells!

Think about this

The Zoma is a chance to meet with friends and buy something special. Wandering under hundreds of parasols, the Malagasy mingle with visitors from all over the world who come to see what this special market has to offer. Have you ever been to a bazaar? If you were a trader at the Zoma, what would you sell and why?

ALL SAINTS' DAY

Celebrated on November 1st by the island's Catholics, All Saints' Day recognizes individuals who have lived holy, devout lives. People attend special services, gather for communal prayers, and bring flowers to cemeteries.

Early to church

In strong Catholic centers, such as Antananarivo, Fianarantsoa, and Tsiroanomandidy, All Saints' Day is a fairly large festival. Parents bring their children to church at dawn to attend mass. The children are dressed in their best clothes and colorful straw hats, eager to place their candles on the church's central altar. Children also help their parents prepare food offerings made into special garlands with which to decorate the saints' statues.

A church at Tsiroanomandidy. Christianity was introduced to Madagascar in the early nineteenth century.

A parade and a meal

Above: Participating in the parade.

As All Saints' Day progresses, many people gather outside the church. A colorful parade of worshipers forms, headed by a statue of the Virgin Mary. Together with statues of other saints, the Blessed Virgin is carried into the church and prominently displayed on the church's central altar. Then, the people sing and pray together.

Below: Remembering loved ones.

Villagers gather up food that was taken to the church the day before and carry it to a communal meeting place. Although this is a religious festival, men drink wine made from cane sugar and rice, while women and children enjoy delicious soft drinks made from oranges and bananas.

THINGS FOR YOU TO DO

There are many stories about animals and plants in Madagascar. Some animals, such as the zebu, are seen elsewhere in Africa but have become special because of their importance during festival celebrations. Read on to find out more about the animals in Madagascar, then tell your friends what you have learned. What is also distinctive about Madagascar are the people, who have a unique sense of dress. Learn how to make a lamba and drape it around yourself!

The wise old tortoise

There is a saying in Mahafaly, "You will never see a tortoise crossing the road during the day." The reason you won't is because anyone coming along the road will take the tortoise with him or her. The tortoise species in Madagascar is both unique and **endangered**. Yet, Mahafaly people still love to eat these animals. During a Mahafaly festival, tortoise meat is an important ingredient of *vary amidanana* [VAAR ame-NAA-nan]. This dish is eaten only on special occasions. It contains herbs, leaves, onions, red peppers, and a special chutney flavoring made from French beans. Which other animals in Madagascar are rare and endangered? Go to your local library and find the answer!

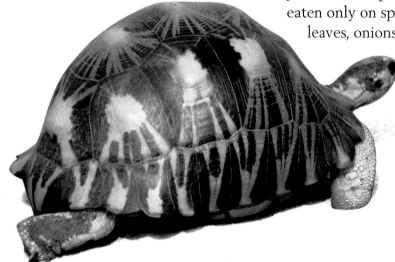

A zebu story

A long time ago in Madagascar, there lived a king who was famous for both the great love he had for his people and his passion for breeding zebu, or humped-back cattle. Near the end of his life in 1809, the king commanded that a huge party be held when he died, instead of mass mourning. When the king died, a great feast was prepared, and the king's loyal subjects ate 3,000 of the king's prized zebu. Since then, the zebu has retained its importance in many Malagasy festivals.

Make your own lamba!

A lamba is a piece of cloth, made of cotton, silk, or **synthetic** materials, worn by Malagasy men and women. A lamba is useful for keeping the sun off the wearer's head and protecting clothes from dust. Men tie lambas around their waists. Women wear them around their shoulders and, sometimes, to cover their heads. If the tail falls on the right side of the body, it signifies that the wearer is in mourning. How can a piece of cloth have a tail? Drape a piece of cloth measuring about 8 feet x 4 feet (2.4 meters x 1.2 meters), the size of a lamba, around your shoulders. Let one of the corners hang down your back. That's the tail! Make one and you'll see.

Things to look for in your library

Chameleon: On Location. Kathy Darling and Tara Darling (Lothrop, Lee and Shepard Books, 1997).

Guide to Madagascar. Hilary Bradt (Globe Pequot, 1997).

Madagascar. (http://embassy.org/madagascar/index.html, 1997).

Madagascar: Green Challenge for the Red Island. (Conservation International, 1995).

Madagascar: A World Out of Time. Frans Lasky, Alwin Jolly, and Gerald Durrell (Aperture, 1990).

Music From the World: Music from Madagascar. (Buda Music, 1992).

Rossy. (Shanachie Entertainment Corp., 1993).

MAKE A RAFFIA COASTER

Raffia is the fiber of the raffia palm, which grows in Madagascar. It is used to make hats and baskets. Buy some raffia at your local craft shop and weave your own coaster.

You will need:
1. Different colored raffia
2. Cardboard
3. A ruler
4. Tape
5. A pair of scissors
6. A wax pencil

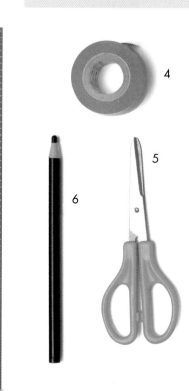

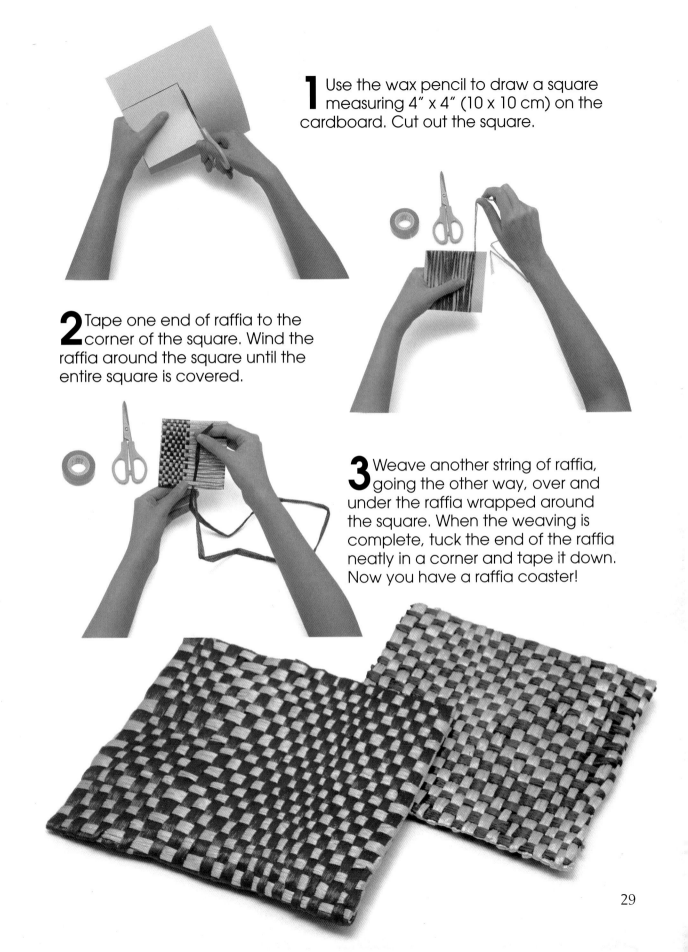

1 Use the wax pencil to draw a square measuring 4" x 4" (10 x 10 cm) on the cardboard. Cut out the square.

2 Tape one end of raffia to the corner of the square. Wind the raffia around the square until the entire square is covered.

3 Weave another string of raffia, going the other way, over and under the raffia wrapped around the square. When the weaving is complete, tuck the end of the raffia neatly in a corner and tape it down. Now you have a raffia coaster!

MAKE A MILKSHAKE

The Malagasy use bananas in many dishes, such as fritters and flambe. Try this milkshake made with bananas, and don't forget to give your milkshake that special Malagasy touch by adding vanilla flavoring and a little coconut.

You will need:
1. 2 cups (480 ml) milk
2. 3 tablespoons of ice cream
3. 1 teaspoon of vanilla powder or extract
4. 1 teaspoon of shredded coconut
5. A spoon
6. Measuring spoons
7. 1 tablespoon honey
8. 1 large banana, cut into pieces
9. About 15 strawberries
10. A blender

1 Put strawberries, banana pieces, honey, and 1 cup (240 ml) of milk into the blender. Blend until smooth.

2 Add ice cream to the mixture. Blend just until mixed.

3 Stir in the rest of the milk, the vanilla extract, and the shredded coconut. Chill your milkshake in the refrigerator, and you'll have a refreshing drink.

GLOSSARY

circumcision, 10	Removal of parts of certain sexual organs in males and females.
converge, 20	Come from different places and meet at one point.
endangered, 26	Few in number and close to extinction.
exhumation, 12	The removal of a body from its burial place.
extolls, 16	Praises.
frantically, 18	Excitedly and with great energy.
glistening, 20	Shining and sparkling.
lambas, 17	Cloth shawls, or wraps, worn by both Malagasy men and women.
oratory, 16	The skill of giving speeches before a large crowd.
spectacles, 20	Unusual and amazing sights.
spellbinding, 3	Captivating and alluring.
synthetic, 27	Man-made; not natural.
tranquilizers, 22	Substances that cause sleepiness or drowsiness.
valiha, 18	A type of zither.
zebu, 9	Cattle with humps on their backs.

INDEX

Picture credits
A. N. A. Press Agency: 17 (bottom); Camera Press: 3 (bottom), 5, 7, 13 (top), 15, 19, 20 (top), 22 (bottom); Ron Emmons: 10 (top); Focus Team-Italy: 10 (bottom); HBL Network: 4, 25 (bottom), 27 (top); Jay Heale: 6 (bottom); Hutchison Library: 9 (both), 18 (top); John R. Jones: 3 (top), 11, 12, 14 (both), 16, 17 (top), 20 (bottom), 22 (top), 23, 24, 25 (top), 26; Pietro Scòzzari: 2, 6 (top), 13 (bottom), 28; Still Pictures: 27 (bottom); Travel Ink: 1; Trip Photographic Agency: 8, 18 (bottom); Topham Picturepoint: 21

Digital scanning by
Superskill Graphics Pte Ltd